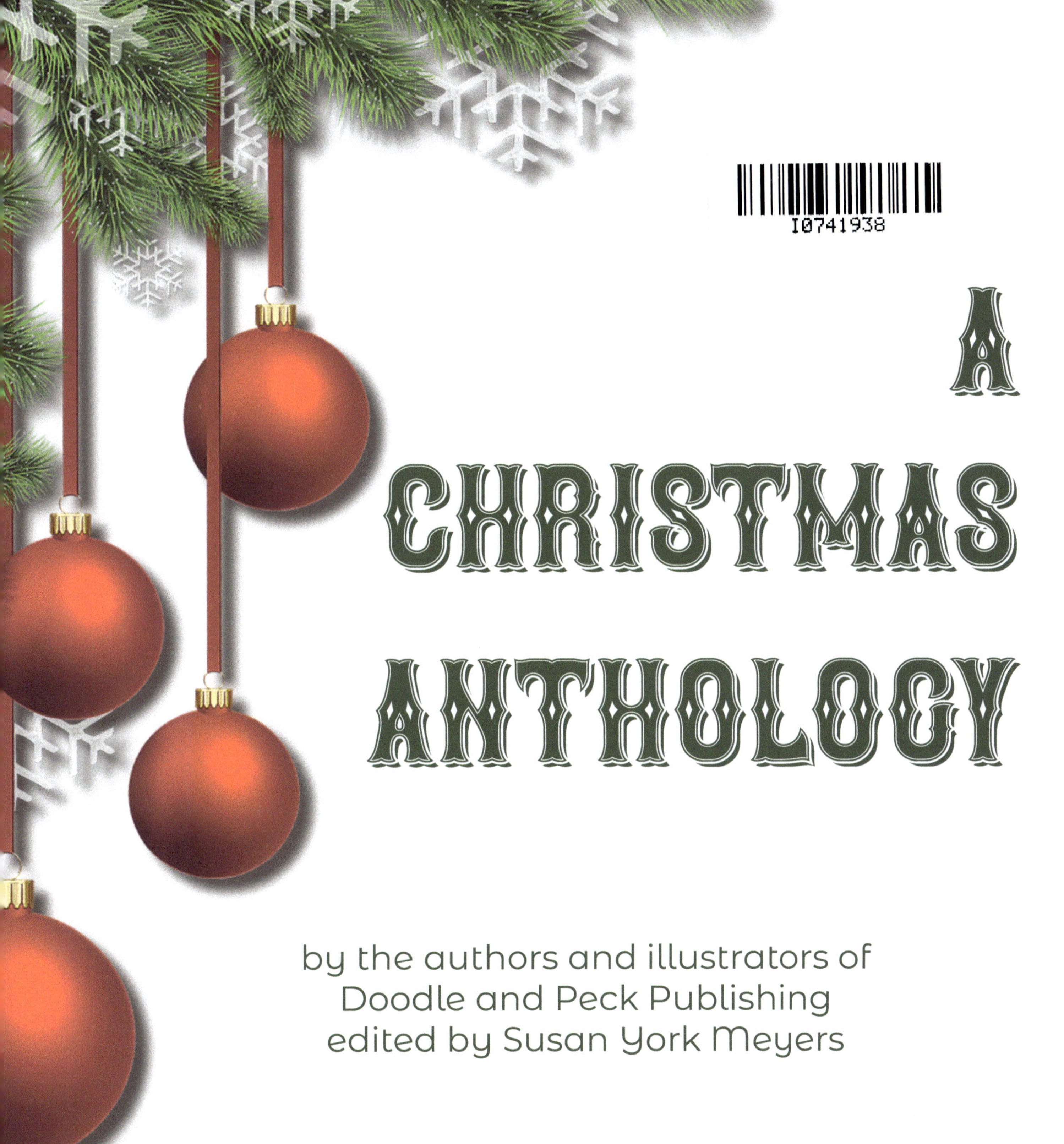


# A CHRISTMAS ANTHOLOGY

by the authors and illustrators of
Doodle and Peck Publishing
edited by Susan York Meyers

Doodle and Peck Publishing
413 Cedarburg Ct.
Yukon, OK 73099
405.354.7422

www.doodleandpeck.com

photographs courtesy of Pixabay

Dedicated to all the diligent, hard working authors and illustrators who never give up. Good luck in all your publishing endeavors!

DOODLE AND PECK PUBLISHING

# Table of Contents

# A Special Treat for Santa

by Darlina Chambers Eichman
illustrations by  Glori Alexander

During Alec's Space Station Vacation, he'd nearly destroyed the entire space station by chewing on a few harmless looking electrical wires. Santa showed up just in time, and he and Alec had fixed all the problems. Santa even gave great spacey gifts to the astronauts and to Alec. What a guy!

This Christmas Eve, Santa would visit Alec the old-fashioned way. Yep. On Earth. Down through the chimney. Alec wanted to give a special gift to Santa. But what? Homemade gifts were always best. Alec was a very good cook. He'd make a treat for Santa. But Santa tasted treats from all over the planet. What could Alec make that would be out of this world? He thought about his favorite treats - cheese and pie. Wait a minute! He had it! He pulled out a recipe card.

This would be the best treat ever. Alec gathered the wet ingredients. He beat together the cream cheese and sweetened condensed milk. He stirred in lemon juice and vanilla. He poured the mixture into the graham cracker crust and spooned the cherry filling on top. Alec stepped back and studied his creation.

"Perfect," he said. There was only one step left. He read the final line which said to chill the cheese pie. FOR AT LEAST ONE HOUR? Oh no. Santa would arrive before it cooled!

What should Alec do? The quickest way to chill food was in the freezer. Alec opened the freezer door. Holiday foods filled it to the brim and the cheese pie wouldn't fit. Giving up on that idea, Alec opened the refrigerator. Having it cool a little bit was better than not at all. He tried to look past the ham, turkey, cranberries and salads but the shelves were too full. Every drawer bulged with festive foods. There was no room in the fridge. Alec closed the door and sat on the edge of the counter. If only he'd started the treat earlier. But he had waited until the last minute. Now Santa would have to eat warm cheese pie.

A shining blue light caught Alec's attention. It came from the early Christmas present the human, Missus, had unwrapped with her family before bed. She had laughed, saying it would help to keep the fridge from being so full again.

If it worked like the fridge, Alec thought, maybe he could use it. He read the sign on the front door.

Ready in a jiffy! What a find! he thought. Jiffy meant fast like rocket speed. He slid the cheese pie into the compartment and turned the dial to 100%.

Alec peeked through the glass. The cherry cheese pie looked funny in there. Was it...shrinking? He didn't remember that happening to cheese pies before. Maybe that's how the new machine cooled things so fast. As he watched, the cheese pie quickly shrank to half its size and then even faster in half again. Panicked, he tried to open the door. Locked!

"Oh, no!" He checked the sign on the machine and read the small print.

"Dehydrator." How had he missed that?

Ding! The machine went still.

"No way!" Alec removed the strangely warm and dry cherry cheese pie. "This is all wrong!"

Just then, sleigh bells rang, and hooves clackety-clicked on the roof.

With no time left, Alec thought he'd better at least taste the treat before giving it to Santa. He broke off a chunk. He nibbled a bite. It reminded him of something he'd eaten before but what? He remembered! It was just like the space food he'd eaten on the space station. He popped the entire piece into his mouth. "Yum," he said. "It has a strong cheesy flavor that finishes nicely with cherry!"

Alec quickly broke the cheese pie into bite-sized chunks and poured them into a bag. He tied a bow onto the package and set it on the table.

Whoosh! Santa appeared. He placed amazing gifts around the tree. "Now, where are the cookies?" Santa curiously picked up Alec's package. "These don't look like cookies." He plucked out a cheesy chunk. He tossed it into the air and caught it in his mouth. He swallowed his treat then glanced at Alec.

"Ho! Ho! Ho!" he called out. "My new favorite. Cherry Cheese Pie Chunks! Next stop...the space station!"

"Mind if I come along?" Alec asked.

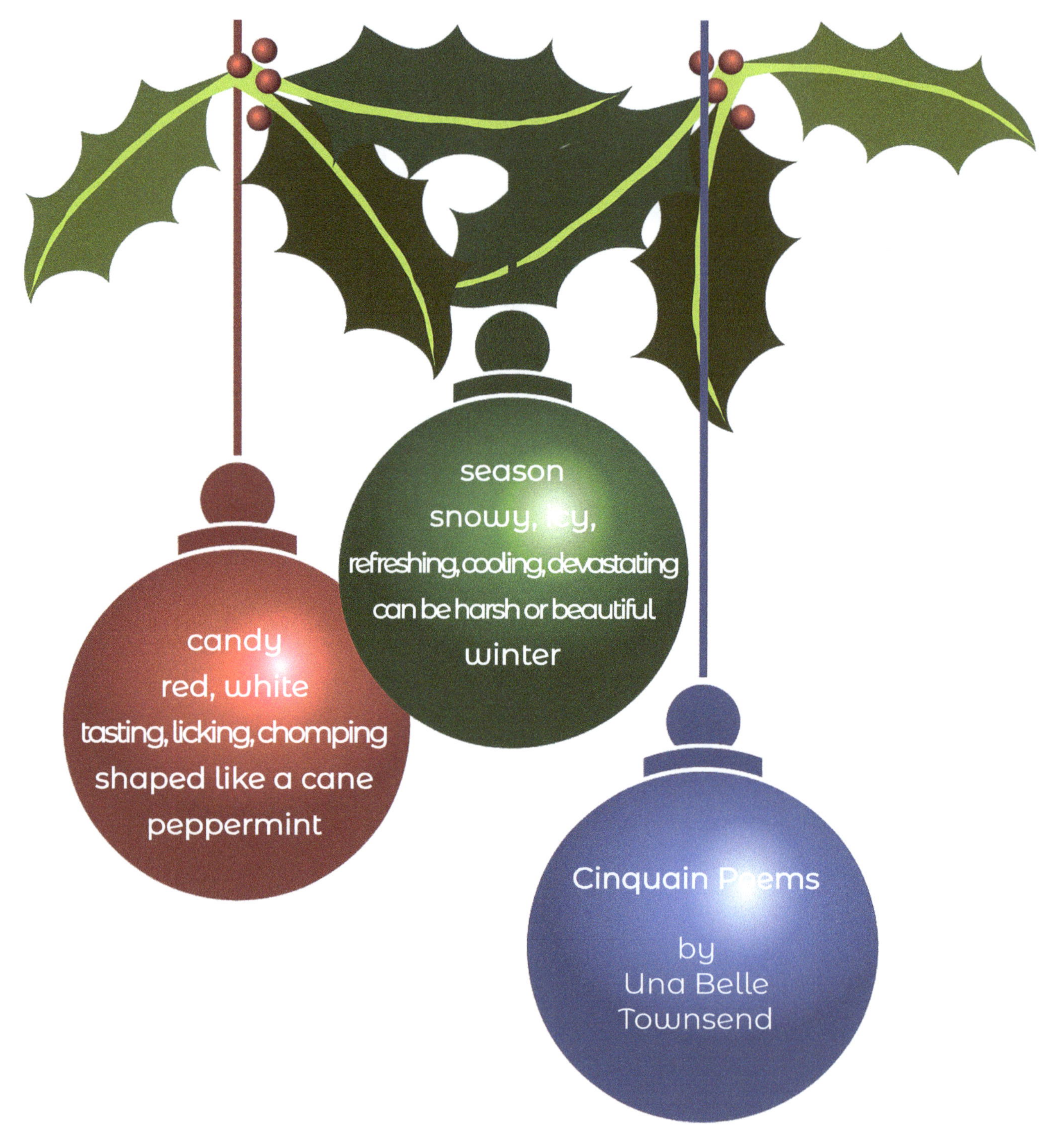
candy
red, white
tasting, licking, chomping
shaped like a cane
peppermint

season
snowy, icy,
refreshing, cooling, devastating
can be harsh or beautiful
winter

Cinquain Poems

by
Una Belle
Townsend

# cinquain poetry

(SIN-cain): an unrhymed poem consisting of five lines arranged in a special way. A cinquain is an example of shape poetry.  Cinquain poems can be written about anything. They are five lines long. The syllable pattern is 2, 4, 6, 8, 2.

1.  Brainstorm ideas first.
2.  Count the syllables.
3.  "Center" your poem on the page.
4.  Rhyme if you want to.
5.  Have fun!

# A Christmas Surprise

by Una Belle Townsend

A few days before Christmas, Mom told my sister we could walk to town and buy one last Christmas present for ourselves. Mom couldn't go with us because the baby was due at any time.

Ruth and I put the dollar bills Mom gave us in our coat pockets and walked to town.

"One more gift under the tree," said Ruth. "I don't know if I need another doll, but I might see one I want."

"I know," I said. "I think I want something different—something no one would think to buy me for Christmas. I probably won't know what it is until I see it."

We waited for cars along the four lane highway to leave, and we finally crossed the busy street. We strolled through many stores trying to decide how to spend our money.

"What are we going to buy?" asked Ruth.

"Do you need a new hat?" I said.

"No, I don't need another one."

"Are you still thinking of that microscope or science kit?" Ruth asked.

"I'm not sure," I said. "Maybe for my birthday."

We kept shopping. It was getting late, and the stores would close soon. Finally, we stopped in front of Wellsey's store. Mother didn't shop there because it was too expensive.

Ruth hesitated. "Would Mom care if we just walked in and looked around?"

"I don't think so." We pushed open the heavy door and stepped inside.

"Wow! Look at all those Christmas trees on the balcony," whispered Ruth. "And those big Christmas wreaths and banners hanging from the ceiling."

"Yum! Cinnamon rolls and gingerbread." I inhaled the spicy fragrance.

"Caramels and taffy, too," Ruth said. "Maybe we should save a little money for something sweet."

Everywhere we looked, there were beautiful gift-wrapped packages and special decorations with blinking lights. We passed gigantic toy displays, and saw Santa in his big green chair. A toy train chugged around the top shelf along one wall. Everything was pretty, big, and expensive.

I looked at a price tag. "These things cost way too much. We'd better leave."

"But we haven't found anything to buy," said Ruth.

"They're too expensive. We can't afford it," I said. "No wonder Mom doesn't shop here."

As we headed toward the front door, Ruth spotted a doll. Even if we pooled our money, we couldn't buy it. A beautiful stuffed cat with green eyes caught my eye, but I didn't have enough for it. We continued toward the big door hoping we'd find something to buy.

"Oooh, look at that sweater," said Ruth. "It feels so soft."

"Too expensive," I said.

"You want a new purse?" she asked.

"Not at that price! Too expensive."

"Oh, look at this doll," said Ruth. "It isn't as much as the other one, and it even comes with extra clothes." She sighed and laid it back in its crib. "I know. It's too expensive."

The store would close in a few minutes, and we needed to get home. As we walked down a side aisle, a sales clerk hung up a sign near a display of jewelry boxes. It said, "Half price!" It was exactly what we had in our pockets! We stopped. I made sure of the price.

"Ruth," I said. "This jewelry box is huge, and it's not too expensive! There's room for lots of necklaces, bracelets, and rings."

"I want one," said Ruth to the clerk. "Blue, please."

I chose a white one.

The sales clerk asked if we wanted them gift-wrapped. "It's free," she said.

We grinned at each other and said, "Yes".

We went to the back counter where volunteers wrapped gifts. We gazed at the rolls of Christmas paper, ribbons, and bows.

"I want the shiny red foil paper with the tiny candy canes on it," said Ruth. "And, I want lots of bows on my package." I wanted the bright green foil paper. It had small Christmas wreaths on it. After looking at all the decorations on the counter, I chose tiny angels and silver bells for the top of my package. We left the store just in time. A store employee locked the doors behind us.

As we carried our big packages home, Ruth said, "I'm glad we found something that wasn't too expensive in that store. Our friends who have small jewelry boxes with dancing ballerinas on them will be jealous."

Our beautifully-wrapped gifts stood out under the tree. We were proud of the special presents we had bought. Mother seemed to approve, too.

On Christmas Eve morning, Dad woke us and said, "Guess what! You have a new baby sister!"

"What's her name?" Ruth asked.

"It's Beth," Dad said.

"When can we see her?" I asked.

"Tonight," he said.

After visiting Mom and Beth at the hospital that evening, Ruth and I begged Dad to let us open just one present. He agreed.

We grabbed our presents with the shiny paper and big bows. We ripped off the paper and showed the jewelry boxes to Dad. He looked at them, grinned, and said, "What are you planning to put in them?"

All of a sudden it hit us. We had big beautiful jewelry boxes, but no jewelry. Not even a ring from a gumball machine!

Dad handed each of us a small box. "Maybe you should open these gifts, too."

We quickly tore off the paper. Inside were tiny birthstone bracelets and rings for each of us. And, a note that said, "Merry Christmas from your new sister, Beth."

# Merry Christmas from Suki and Sam!

by author Dr. Lisa Marotta and illustrator, Dorothy Shaw

# The Twelve Days of Christmas

by David Barrow

# 1
## PARTRIDGE
### PEAR TREEING

# 2
## TURTLE
### DOVES

"REALLY?   YOU'RE JUST GONNA LEAVE ME
STUCK OUT HERE ALONE?
THIS IS SUPPOSED TO BE A LOVE SONG,  YA KNOW.
YOU HOOKED THOSE TWO DOVES UP.
WHAT'S UP WITH THAT?   HUH?
THAT'S PROFILING, THAT'S WHAT THAT IS!

I TELL YOU WHAT."

3
FRENCH
HENS
"AND OO-LA-LA TO YOU."

4
BiRDS
CALLING

5
GOLD
RiNGS

"OKAY, THAT'S 5 RiNGS.  GET READY."

6
GEESE
LAYING

7
SWANS
SWIMMING

8
MAiDS
MiLKiNG
"TOO MANY!  WAY - TOO - MANY!"

9
LADIES
DANCING
"YOUNG LADIES DO NOT DANCE!"

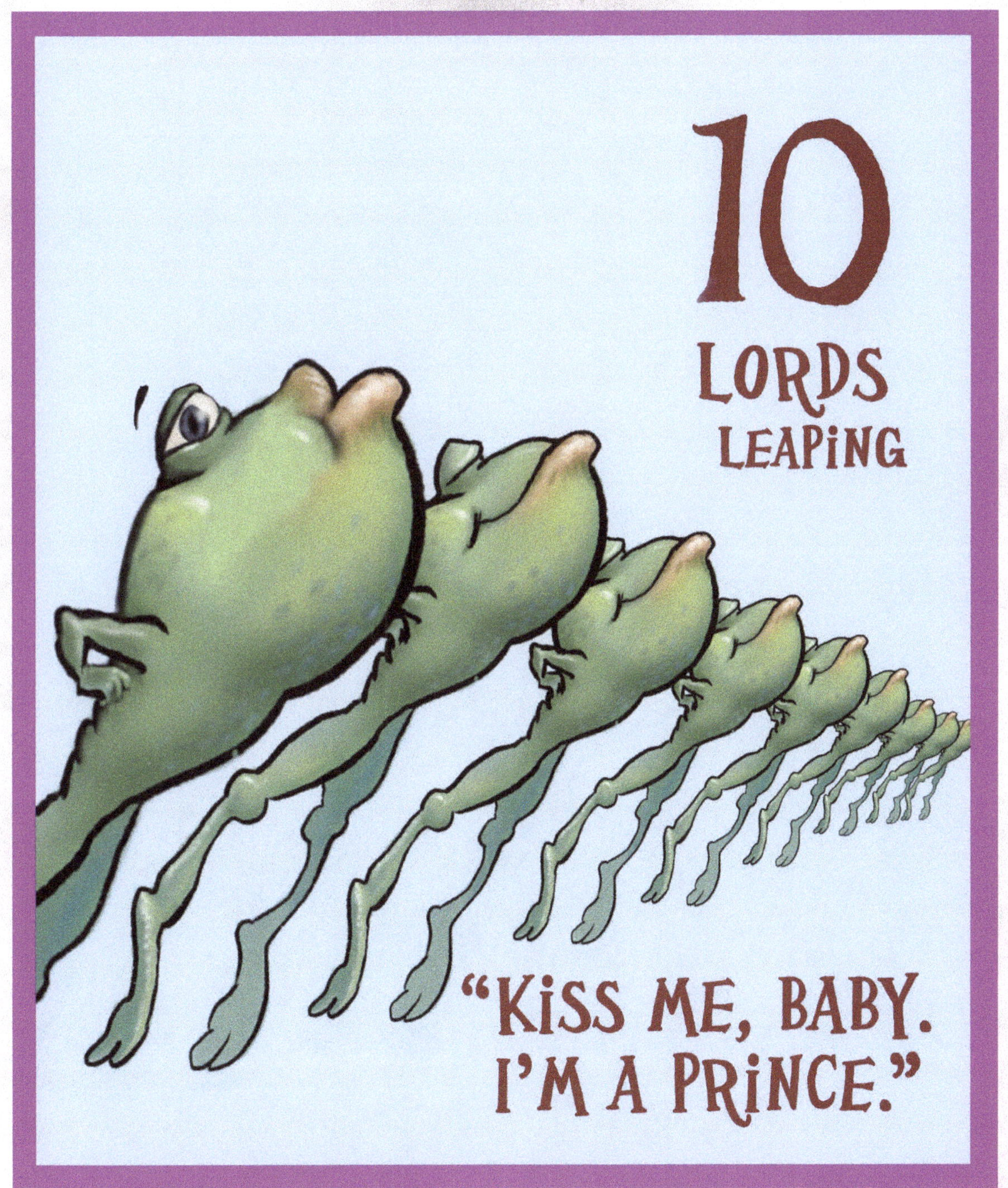

10
LORDS LEAPING
"KISS ME, BABY. I'M A PRINCE."

11
PIPERS
PIPING
"YOU MEAN
11 PLUMBERS HAVE WORKED ON THIS
AND it STILL LEAKS?!"

12
DRUMMERS
DRUMMING
COULDN'T FIND 12 DRUMMERS,
BUT I SCROUNGED UP 12 DRUMS.

# Mila Denton's Christmas Wish

## by Sandra Byrd Lawson

Only seven days until Christmas! I crossed all my fingers and toes (even my extra pinky toe) and wished for a puppy. Every time I asked Mom, she said, "Mila, a dog is a huge responsibility." I knew what she really meant. No dog. But I'm NOT a little kid like last year. I can take care of a dog, and a dog is the only thing I'd asked Santa to bring.

At school, Miss Allen said we were bouncing off the walls. I'm not exactly sure how kids do that. Especially since we mostly hadn't left our seats. For the past week, parents had brought in treats every day. And every morning on the intercom, the announcer person said, "Merry Christmas, Garrett Elementary!"

To top it all off, everyone was being super nice. Like the song says, Santa sees you when you're bad or good, so be good for goodness sake. Tony Baloney had to work extra hard at it. Probably because he was the baddest kid in the whole, entire class. And he knew it.

After math, Miss Allen walked over to the calendar and made a big red X across today's date. "Two more days of school. Does everyone have exciting plans?" The room suddenly sounded like a bunch of bees buzzing. "Shhh! Everyone will have a chance."

Miss Allen smoothed her hair back. "I'm going to visit my family in Texas. We'll decorate the tree, do a lot of shopping and baking, and sing Christmas carols." Her eyes turned all dreamy looking. "Spending the holidays with my family is the only thing I want for Christmas." She looked around the class. "Now, we'll take turns today and tomorrow. You can tell what you want for Christmas or what your plans are for our holiday break."

Rosie raised her hand. "I've already gone to the mall to see Santa. I asked him for a Baby Brittany video game. I'm pretty sure I'm gonna get it."

"Went to see Santa?" Tony Baloney hollered. "Baby Brittany for Baby Rosie! I bet you even sat on Santa's lap like a baby. Wah! Wah!" He pooched out his bottom lip and rubbed his eyes like he was crying.

"That's quite enough, Anthony!" Miss Allen scolded. "One more disruption and you'll visit Principal Wrigley. Wouldn't that be terrible so close to the holidays?"

Tony Baloney's ears turned fire engine red. He scooted down in his seat. "Yes, Miss Allen."

I felt sorry for Rosie. Tony Baloney can be a real meanie-butt. Just because you go see Santa doesn't mean you're a baby. I'd do almost anything for a puppy. But, now I'd have to make sure no one from school saw me sitting on Santa's lap. Especially Tony Baloney.

On the school bus, Tony Baloney gave Rosie the stink eye. Then he said to Jeannette, "Bet you're gonna go see Santa Claus, too. Gonna sit on his knee and give him your baby Christmas list." He laughed and pointed at her. "Baby Jeannette. Baby, baby, ba-beee." Jeannette's eyes filled with tears.

Next thing I knew, Jeannette's big brother turned around and said, "Hey, you little pipsqueak. Leave my sister alone. If you don't knock it off, I'm going to feed you a sandwich." He made a fist and shook it in Tony Baloney's face. "A knuckle sandwich. Get it, Baloney Boy?"

Tony Baloney gulped. He didn't say another word. I'm pretty sure he's on Santa's Naughty List.

When I got home from school, Mom said we were going to the mall to see Santa. Really? I wanted to be excited. But after today, I had the collywobbles. That's what Grandma says when she's nervous about something.

My little sister squealed. "See Santa. My Santa. "

Mom smiled all over the place. "Katie Ann, are you going to sit on Santa's lap and tell him what you want for Christmas?"

Katie Ann's eyes bugged out like she'd seen a giant spider. She stood like a statue for a minute thinking about what Mom asked. Then she shook her head. "No, Mommy. Nooooooo." She hid her face in Mom's chest.

"Mila can show you how it's done. Can't you, Mila?"

Just like that, an idea popped into my brain. I'd go hold Katie Ann's hand and then I'd whisper to Santa about the puppy. No one would ever know. Brilliant!

That night after supper, Dad drove Mom and us to the mall. I chewed my nails into nubs on the way. The parking lot was so packed, we practically walked from the next town over. It was freezing cold. Katie Ann and I were bundled up like human burritos. Every time I breathed out, it looked like a puff of smoke rising up in front of my face. We pretended to be fire-breathing dragons all the way to the mall entrance. That helped us forget our fingers and toes had turned into ice cubes.

When we finally got inside, my jaw dropped. "Gee whiz!" I whined. "Look at that line! We won't see Santa Claus until next Christmas."

Katie Ann started to cry. Mom frowned at me. "Mila's joking," she said as she wiped the tears from Katie Ann's cheeks. "Look, the line's moving already. Santa won't leave tonight until he's seen all the children that are waiting. I promise."

Mom held our hats and gloves at the back of the line. Katie Ann and I inched closer to Santa. I watched Dad sneak away to do some secret shopping, but he walked right past the pet store and didn't even look inside. I eyed the crowd. Thank goodness, I didn't see a single kid from Garrett Elementary. We stood for almost forever. Finally, I counted one, two, three, four. Only four more ahead of us!

"What are you going to ask Santa for, Katie Ann?"

"I get big princess palace. And Priscilla Pony and Princess Piper."

"I bet Santa will bring it. You've been a good girl this year. One, two, three." I counted again. "Only three more in front of us."

I was so close, I could actually hear Santa talking to some kid. But something was weird. Very weird.

I stared hard. I thought my eyes would jump out of my head. I rubbed them. Twice. Was I dreaming? There was Tony Baloney sitting right on Santa's lap. Unbelievable!

"I want a new basketball goal for my house and some Johnny Flyer basketball shoes, Sir."

"Well, Anthony. Have you been a good boy all year?" Santa asked.

"As good as I can be."

"Well, it seems I remember some incidents that occurred at school this year," Santa said. He scratched his chin. "You've played some pretty rotten tricks on your classmates. Have you made amends for your actions?"

"Amends?"

Santa cleared his throat. "Have you changed your ways? Have you made up for all the trouble you've caused?"

Tony Baloney hung his head. "I've spent a lot of time in the principal's office. And I've missed a few days of recess. And I've written a lot of sentences like 'I will not make fun of Mila's extra toe' one hundred times."

Santa chuckled. "Well, Christmas will be here before you know it. If you can keep your nose clean, uh, I mean if you can behave, maybe you'll get what you're asking for. Now, run along. I have many more children to see before I go feed my reindeer."

I still couldn't believe my eyes or ears. Tony Baloney hopped off Santa's knee and started to walk away. Our eyes locked. He gulped. I grinned. I had the goods on him and he knew it.

When it was finally our turn, Katie Ann and I stepped up. "Mila Denton! Well, well, well. It's always good to see you," Santa said. "And little Katie Ann. How are you, girls? Are you ready to tell me what you want for Christmas?"

"I'm just here with Katie Ann," I stammered.

Santa's eyebrows shot up. I winked at him.

Katie Ann had watched about a million kids in line. How could she still be afraid? Santa's helper lifted her onto Santa's lap. "She wants me to hold her hand," I said. The man in the elf suit stepped aside.

"Well, little Miss Katie Ann. What a big girl you are. Last year, you wouldn't even look at me. Did you like your gifts?"

Katie Ann nodded and her bottom lip pooched out. Her chin quivered. I just knew she'd wail any minute.

"Now, I know you've been a good girl. What are you asking for this year?"

Katie Ann looked up at me. "Tell him what you want, Katie Ann," I said. "There are other kids here, too. Santa's really busy."

Katie Ann looked at all the kids in line, then she blurted out her list. Santa nodded. Before he sat her down, I leaned over and whispered, "I'm sorry, Santa. I can't sit on your knee this year, but I want a puppy. A real, live puppy. That's all."

Santa frowned. "Do you know how many children ask for a pet for Christmas and they don't take care of it? It's a terrible thing, Mila. A pet is a big responsibility. And I think your mother has said no every time you've asked. Am I right?"

"You're right that Mom said no. You're wrong if you think I won't take care of it. I will. I'm not a baby anymore. Please, please bring a puppy. I won't ask for anything for the next five Christmases."

"Five Christmases?" He chuckled. "Mila, you know I won't bring a gift that your parents don't approve of. Let me think about how to handle this. Maybe I can convince them to change their minds, but no promises. Deal?"

"Deal." I didn't know whether to feel good about my talk with Santa or go home and crawl under my bed.

We waited for Dad to meet us after he finished his shopping. None of his packages wiggled or barked.

Katie Ann chattered all the way home. Her story grew and grew until she said, "Santa's going to bring me all the toys in the world."

When Katie Ann finally stopped to catch her breath, Dad said, "So Katie Ann had a good visit with Santa. Mila, how about you?"

I stared out at the streetlights. "I don't want to talk about it," I grumped.

Tony Baloney was the first kid I saw the next day. He was picking on a boy that was littler than him. When he saw me, the color drained from his face and he broke out in a sweat.

I smiled from ear to ear. Then I sang,

"He sees you when you're sleeping.
He knows when you're awake.
He knows when you've been baaaaddd or good.
So be good for goodness sake."

A day later, I felt like I was floating on air. Miss Allen had told us since it was the last day before Christmas break, we wouldn't have any classwork. We were going to watch the fifth graders do a play, and the fourth graders sing Christmas songs. And our class was going to read The Night Before Christmas. My part was the very last sentence. I'd had the brilliant idea that after I said the last word, I'd rat out Tony Baloney. Right there on stage! I couldn't have planned it any better. I was sure Tony Baloney expected me to get him sometime today, but he didn't know exactly when it was coming.

Before lunch, Miss Allen said, "Does anyone else want to tell their Christmas plans or what they've asked for?"

I watched the hands shoot up. Mine was first, of course.

"Okay, Mila. Come on up front so we can see you."

I hopped out of my seat and flew to the front of the room. Tony Baloney and I locked eyes. He was shaking in his shoes. I giggled under my breath. But before I could say a word, Tony Baloney said, "Miss Allen, I don't feel well. May I be excused?"

"My goodness, Anthony. You look pale." Miss Allen put her hand on his forehead.

"You don't feel feverish, but maybe you should go see the school nurse."

He didn't waste a minute getting out of there.

"I've asked for a puppy this year," I announced.

Every single kid in Room 1-B moaned. Then Johnny Marcum said, "Forget it, Mila. Everyone asks for a puppy and no one gets one. I've asked for the past three years, but Mom says I can't have one until I'm married."

"That's right!" Rosie said. "I gave up two Christmases ago. Ain't never gonna happen, Mila."

"All right, children," Miss Allen said. "Mila can ask for whatever she wants. It's up to Santa and her parents if she gets a puppy or not. We won't know until Christmas morning."

"Did you get a puppy when you were a kid, Miss Allen?" Jeannette asked.

"I didn't ask for a puppy," she answered. "My dream was a pony." Miss Allen paused a minute then frowned. "And I never got one."

It felt like a storm cloud had floated over Room 1-B. Four other kids told what they wanted for Christmas, and one kid told us that her family doesn't believe in Christmas at all. I felt really depressed after that.

Later, Tony Baloney came back into our classroom. He sure didn't look sick. But he hadn't said more than two words all day. We did crafts and ate cookies and punch. Tony Baloney stuffed his pockets with cookies when Miss Allen was talking to one of the parents. I was almost positive he'd never make it off the naughty list.

The intercom blared. "It's almost time for our program. Please get ready to file into the gym."

We scrambled to the gym. It was beautiful. The stage had green and red streamers and a huge Christmas tree. I sat on the bleachers with all of Room 1-B and watched the program until Mrs. Wallace motioned for all of us to follow her. We huddled behind the curtain.

Mrs. Wallace took the microphone. "For the final presentation, Room 1-B will read The Night Before Christmas." Everyone clapped as we all walked onto the stage. My stomach felt like a whole butterfly family was inside it. I actually thought I might throw up. Right. There.

I took my place and waited for my part. My knees knocked together like they were playing The Little Drummer Boy, which normally would've been pretty cool. Now it was just embarrassing.

My eyes scanned the crowd. Hey, there's Mom! And Katie Ann! All the sudden, I didn't feel scared or nervous.

While I stood listening to the other kids, I thought about how cool it was going to be to tell all of Garrett Elementary what a two-faced, low-down, dirty double-crosser Tony Baloney was.

Everyone would laugh and point at him. Everyone would think I was the greatest thing since chili and oatmeal candy. I felt all warm inside. My mind drifted. It was like a movie playing before my eyes. The mall. Santa. How nice kids at school were being. A puppy. He sees you when you're sleeping…

I knew what I had to do.

A sharp elbow hit me in the ribs. "Mila!"

"Hey! Knock it off, Rosie!" The whole auditorium burst out in giggles.

"It's your turn!" Rosie whispered.

My eyes widened. My heart raced. It got deathly quiet. Then Katie Ann yelled from the audience. "Hi, Mila! I see you!" Everyone laughed again. Oh, brother.

Out of the corner of my eye, I saw Tony Baloney trying to leave the stage. Mrs. Wallace pointed him back to his spot. His face looked white and pasty. Maybe he really was sick.

I breathed in deep and recited, 'I heard him exclaim as he rode out of sight, Merry Christmas to all (even you, Tony Baloney), and to all a good night'. I looked at Mrs. Wallace and her crinkled forehead. I hoped I wouldn't be in trouble.

The audience clapped and clapped. They even stood up and clapped some more. Then Principal Wrigley took the microphone. "Thank you all for coming and have a wonderful break. We'll see you back on January fourth."

As I walked to our car, Tony Baloney hollered, "Hey, Mila!" I stopped dead in my tracks.

"I'll meet you at the car, Mom," I said. Mom nodded. She and Katie Ann walked away.

"Why'd you do it?" Tony Baloney asked. "Why on earth were you nice to me, Mila?"

I turned up my nose. "I don't know what you're talking about."

"Sure you do. I know you saw me at the mall. How come you didn't tell? You know you wanted to."

"You're right, Tony Baloney. I did want to. And you would totally deserve it. But it's Christmas and time to spread good cheer and all that stuff. Besides, I know Santa's watching. I can't mess up any chance I have at getting a puppy."

"You still hanging on to that dumb wish for a puppy? Everyone knows Santa doesn't bring puppies to kids."

I pursed my lips and stomped my foot. "Tony Baloney! You don't know everything!" I marched all the way to the car.

As we drove away, I saw Tony Baloney trying to flag us down. Mom stopped and I rolled down the window. "What do you want now?" I snapped.

He grinned real big. "I just wanted to tell ya 'Merry Christmas'."

I thought my ears would shrivel up and fall off. "Merry Christmas, Tony Baloney."

The car rolled away while he yelled at the top of his lungs, "I HOPE YOU GET YOUR PUPPY!"

Mom glared at me. "Puppy? Really Mila. I think we've already had this discussion."

Katie Ann squealed from the backseat. "Puppy! Mila get puppy!"

I was as good as a sugar cookie the rest of the time before Christmas. Anything Mom or Dad asked me to do, I did right away. I played dolls with Katie Ann and pretended to be her pony. Mom and Dad didn't have to ask twice for anything.

"My goodness. Someone is really on her best behavior. Does this have anything to do with a certain holiday coming on December twenty-fifth?" asked Mom.

I grinned real big. "Maybe. Can I set the table for supper now?"

Our tree was all decorated except for the star on top. That was the bestest part. And I really, really wanted to be the one to put it up. Dad would lift me onto his shoulders like he always did and it would end in a tickle fest. This year, Katie Ann started squalling as soon as she saw the star. "I do it! I do it!"

"It's okay," I mumbled. "Let Katie Ann do it."

Mom looked at Dad. "Can you believe that? Mila's going to let Katie Ann put the star on top without a fuss?"

Dad shook his head. I guess he was speechless. Then he turned to Katie Ann and said, "How about Mila does the star and you hang this blue ornament right under it. It's a very special ornament." Dad twirled the ornament in front of Katie Ann. She thought for a minute before she yelled, "Okay!"

After the star and ornament were on the tree and the tickle fest was over, Mom whispered to me, "Thank you for offering to let Katie Ann do the star. I know how special that tradition is to you and Dad." She pushed my hair behind my ear. "You're getting so big." Mom sniffled. "You'll be all grown up before we know what's happened."

After church Christmas Eve night, Mom made the whole family wear ugly matching pajamas that Grandma had sent. And, of course, we had to take a picture to prove we actually wore them. Then Mom made hot chocolate while Dad read Christmas stories. Katie Ann and I begged until they let us each open one present.

"Oh, my word! Look at the time." Dad yawned as he looked at his watch. "You girls better get to bed. Santa should be heading this way. But if you're awake, he may not stop. Brush your teeth and we'll tuck you both in."

I didn't wait for Mom and Dad. I flew up the steps, brushed my teeth, and jumped in bed. I squinched my eyes tight and pretended to be asleep. Dad came in, straightened my covers, kissed my forehead, and whispered, "Good night, Doodlebug. Merry Christmas."

I opened one eye. "Merry Christmas, Daddy."

Then I didn't move a muscle. I'd planned to lie very still and hear Santa come down the chimney. Maybe I'd even hear the reindeer on the roof!

The next thing I knew, the sun was peeking through my window. I threw the covers back and hollered, "IT'S CHRISTMAS! WAKE UP, EVERYBODY!"

It sounded like a herd of elephants running down the stairs. I couldn't wait to see my new puppy! I'd been really good, and it was the only thing I'd asked for. Why wouldn't I get it? There were all sizes and shapes of packages under the tree. Big and small. Tall and short. Shiny paper, ribbons, bows. What a sight to see! I stood for a second just to let it sink in. All those presents! Then it dawned on me, none of them were moving. None were barking. None were whining. And none had air holes in them. My heart sank.

Dad used an empty wrapping tube to yell through. His voice sounded funny. "Let the Christmas festivities begin!"

Mom read the names on the packages and stacked them up around us. It was amazing! Some were from Santa and some were from Mom and Dad. Katie Ann and I tore through them pretty fast. Could there possibly be a puppy in one? Katie Ann got exactly what she asked Santa for. I had some pretty cool things. But no puppy. I wanted to sneak back to my room and hide in my closet for a while.

"Mila, honey, what's the matter?" Mom asked.

"Didn't you get what you asked for?" Dad asked.

I shook my head. "I was good as I could be. All I asked for was a puppy." Tears trickled down my cheeks. "I'm big enough to take care of a dog." Sniffle. "I'd love him." Sniffle. "And feed him." Sniffle. "And take him for walks." Sniffle. Mom handed me a tissue for my nose. "I'd show you all. IF I had the chance."

I buried my face in Mom's chest. She hugged me tightly. "Oh, sweetie. I'm so sorry. The last few weeks, you've really proven how mature you are. You really are ready for a dog. I don't know why Santa didn't bring one. Maybe next year. You and Katie Ann will be even older then."

I curled into a little ball behind the Christmas tree. I didn't want to see anyone.

We were startled when the doorbell rang. "Oh, dear. Who on earth can that be?" Mom asked. "Look at this mess!" She snatched wrapping paper off the floor and shoved it behind the sofa.

Dad laughed. "Isn't it too early in the morning for carolers?" He eased the door open.

"Who is it?" Mom called.

"I'm not sure."

By now, I was curious about what was going on. I crawled out from behind the tree and peeked around Dad at the front porch. "This is really weird," Dad said.

I saw a big box with a name scribbled on top. I read it. "Mila Denton." I did a jumping-bean dance. "It says Mila Denton on the tag! That's me!"

"Let's bring it inside," Dad said.

I nodded. Mom's eyes were wide. Katie Ann squealed.

"Well, Mila. Let's see what's inside," Dad said.

I didn't waste any time ripping the paper. It was easy 'cause it already had holes in it. I pulled the lid off the box and squealed. "A puppy. A real, live puppy!"

He had the shiniest black and tan hair and long skinny legs. His collar was blue and red with a gold tag that said Alfie, Property of Mila Denton. I scooped him up and hugged him. He licked my face and grunted. "Where did he come from?"

Dad shrugged his shoulders. Mom glared at him. I ran to the door and looked out. There were boot prints that led across the yard. I jumped into my winter boots and followed them all the way to where they disappeared. Right into thin air!

When I got back inside, Dad said, "This might answer your questions. Inside the box is everything you need to get started. A leash, a bed, food, bowls, and in the very bottom, a note."

*Dear Mila,*

*You've been a good girl this year, especially the last couple of weeks. I know you are old enough for a puppy now and your parents agree. Alfie is the perfect match for you.*

*I'm sorry this box is a little late. It got misplaced in the sled and went all the way back to the North Pole with me.*

*Take good care of this little guy. He's a very special pooch.*

*Remember, I'm always watching.*

*Santa C.*

I flipped out. I couldn't stop smiling. Alfie had some toys and I showed him how to tug. He tugged and tugged, then he stopped and ran to the corner and left a little yellow puddle.

Mom rolled her eyes. "Mila. He's your dog."

"Yep. That's right. He's my dog," I answered. "And he's the bestest dog in the whole world."

# Nonets

by Susan York Meyers



by Marla F. Jones

38

Definition: A nonet is a nine-line poem, beginning with nine syllables on the first line, and decreasing by one syllable each following line. The nonets on this page are inverted to give a Christmas tree shape to the poem.

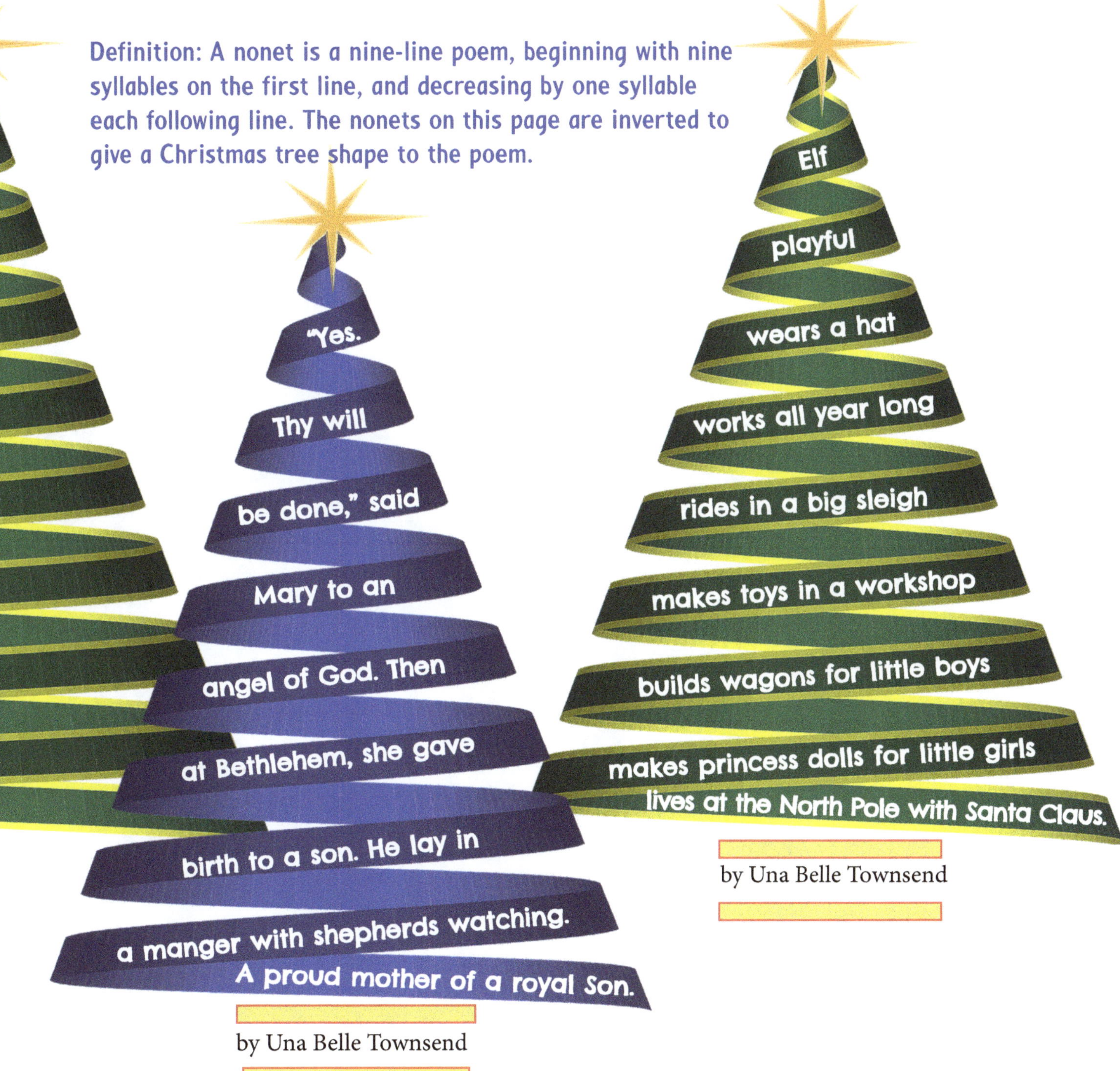


by Una Belle Townsend

by Una Belle Townsend

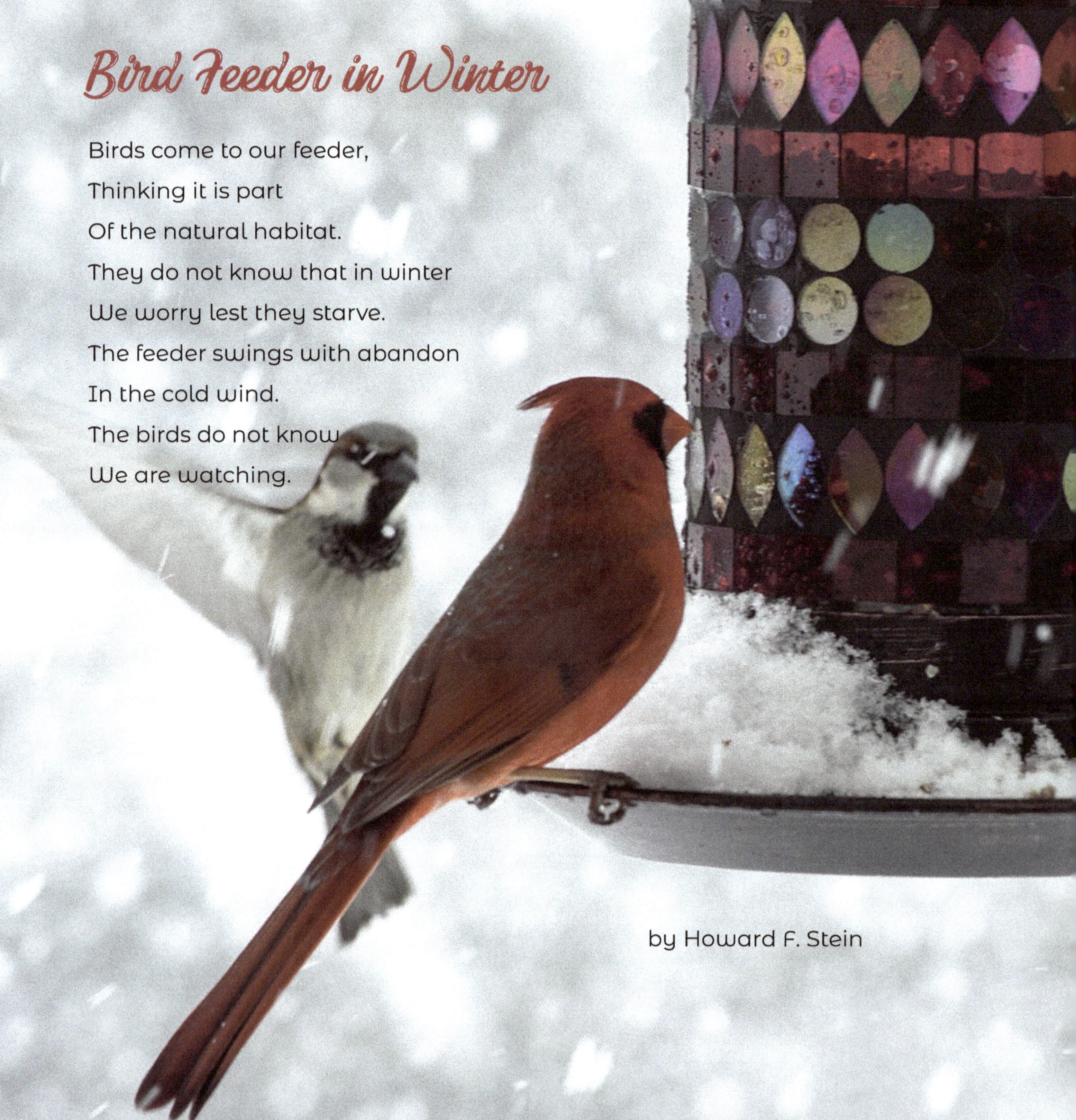
Bird Feeder in Winter

Birds come to our feeder,
Thinking it is part
Of the natural habitat.
They do not know that in winter
We worry lest they starve.
The feeder swings with abandon
In the cold wind.
The birds do not know
We are watching.

by Howard F. Stein

# Jerome the Snowstone*

# Seeing Santa

by Susan Meyers

Sometimes adults forget a child's reality is a magical place, a fragile place. It can easily be taken away by grownups who have forgotten how to believe. But every so often, a grownup is privileged to get a quick peek into that world.

One freezing February, my fellow teachers and I bundled up the preschoolers from our daycare and escorted them to a local bakery. Christmas was but a winter memory, so it wasn't visions of sugarplums dancing in small heads. Instead, dreams of the promised cupcake treats filled their thoughts as we navigated through the front door. Our stomachs growled as the enticing smell of cinnamon and sugar tickled our noses.

"Santa Claus!"

"It's Santa Claus!"

Puzzled, I glanced around. The kids ignored displays of pastry delights, including the promised cupcakes, and rushed to crowd around a small table. Then I spotted him, a white haired, long-bearded gentleman smiling at the wide-eyed children.

"Where are your reindeer, Santa?"

"I left them at home."

"Where's your red suit, Santa?"

"It's after Christmas so I don't wear it." The old gentleman pushed his coffee aside. He leaned down, elbows on his knees in order to be face to face with even the smallest tot.

"Will you bring us toys again, Santa?"

"You bet."

"Will you say, 'ho, ho, ho, Santa?'"

"If you'll say it with me."

"Ho, ho, ho's," filled the scented air, Santa's being the loudest and the merriest.

This jolly man not only entered the fragile, magical reality of a child's imagination, but he left it safely intact.

That day, Santa became my hero.

# Granny's Gifts

by Barbara Shepherd

The Air Force delivered our last box of household stuff last week so we could finally watch TV after getting our phone and cable connected. We'd been waiting on that last shipment for three weeks to reach our rent house, off base this time. We'd been in England and Guam for four years, and my brother and I didn't know anyone here in northern Oklahoma except my dad's grandma.

When the landline rang, I jumped. The receiver looked like the cable remote when I found it. "Hello."

"Is this Connor?"

"Yes."

"Come over tomorrow," Granny said, her voice scratchy over the phone. "I have your Christmas gift, Connor. Bring an air compressor and a car vacuum."

Oh, no. That meant strings attached.

"I know what you're thinking," she said. "You're right. I'm not mailing you a check this time – now that you're back from overseas. So happy to have all of you back in the states."

"Okay, Granny. I'll be over by middle of the afternoon."

"Make it one o'clock." She hung up.

Guess I'd show up at one or I wouldn't get my cash gift this year. I stretched out on the sofa and started playing games on my phone. I loved Christmas break.

The next afternoon, my older brother and I pulled into Granny's driveway and parked. Racing the engine and listening to the exhaust were bonus points for riding with Roger who just got his driver's license last month. He killed the engine when Granny opened her garage door. She laid her purse on a step stool inside the one-car garage. Her house reminded me of the fairy tale houses in kids' picture books – small and neat with everything in its place.

After I got out, and Granny and I gave each other a hug, she pointed to her old pea-green vehicle, parked in the drive. "The keys are in it." She hugged Roger and sat on the porch swing with him.

I walked over and lifted the heavy hood of the 1950 Ford coupe. I'd never seen so much open space under a hood before. The slant-six motor sat off to the side.

"Well," Granny said, "there's no mystery about it. Just change the oil like your daddy showed you, and air up the tires. I've got places to go."

Where does an old lady need to go? And more importantly, should she be driving at ninety?

"I'm reading your mind," she said. "Of course, I'm driving at ninety, and I'm driving 90. No lolly-gagging for me."

She must have seen the question on my face – a poker face I do not own. My great-grandma flying down the road – at 90 miles an hour.

"Not down the road," she said. "To go 90, you need to be on a paved track."

What? And could she really read my mind?

She and Roger brought me a filter and some oil while I aired up her tires with Roger's little compressor. Then, she showed him her flower beds where rose bushes had been cut back and new mulch put down. "I'll need some help from you two with weeding when spring comes."

After I finished her oil change, I vacuumed out her car with the cool car vac and put it and the air compressor back in Roger's trunk.

"That'll do," she said and picked up her purse. She handed Roger a gift card. "My friend just bought the convenience store on the corner. I put a hundred bucks on this card for your Christmas gift. Figured you could use gas money."

"Thank you, Granny," Roger said. "That's a perfect gift."

Granny got in her car and yelled, "Follow me."

I hopped back into Roger's sporty Camaro. We had trouble keeping up with her.

"That old lady," he said, "can drive! Not just drive fast but she takes corners like a race car driver."

She slowed enough to pull into a parking lot and waved us up beside her. "Park that slow ride of yours. I'll buy lunch and see about that gift."

"How come," I asked Roger, "I had to work for my Christmas gift, and you didn't?"

He laughed and said, "Pays to be the first great-grandchild, I guess."

After we parked, the three of us walked into an Italian restaurant, sat down in a booth, and waited for service. That smell made me wonder if I could wait for food to be cooked. I didn't realize how hungry I was.

"I think I'll try your pizza today, Connor," Granny said. "You did say you wanted Canadian bacon and pineapple."

My mouth flew open so I could say no, but the words never came. Not because I wanted something different, but because I hadn't told anyone my favorite pizza had changed. Pepperoni had always been my choice – until two weeks ago. Wow. Granny must have some kind of powers – a gift maybe?

After the girl took our order, she brought our drinks and salads.

Peeling off a hundred-dollar bill from her stash, Granny handed me the crisp bill and said, "Merry Christmas."

"Thanks for the money, Granny. It'll help me out with my car fund. I hope to have enough saved by the time I turn sixteen."

"Good choice," she said. "You have time to build up that fund. Maybe mow yards next summer."

I tried not to frown. I hated yard work but wanted to have my own car.

A short while later, we made a large pizza disappear.

"Thanks for the lunch, Granny," Roger and I said at the same time.

She smiled and laid cash on the table with the ticket. All of a sudden, she stood and hugged Roger and me. "I love you boys."

I saw tears making her eyes shiny. "I love you, too, Granny."

Roger patted her back. "We love you, Granny. We're getting everything unpacked in our house."

"Don't be strangers," she said. "I shouldn't have to come up with excuses to get you two to come over and visit me."

"Oh, no worries." I kissed her cheek. "We're going to Mom's side of the family for Christmas, but we'll be over to see you as soon as we get back in town."

"You will?"

"Uh-huh. We don't want to miss out on your holiday candies. Do you still make divinity?"

"I do."

"And color it green and pink?"

"Yes. You remembered."

Roger chimed in. "How about potato candy? I love that."

"Yes, and I'll have chocolate fudge and Hawaiian candy, too."

"Yum," he said.

"Yum for me, too. What can we bring you for Christmas, Granny?"

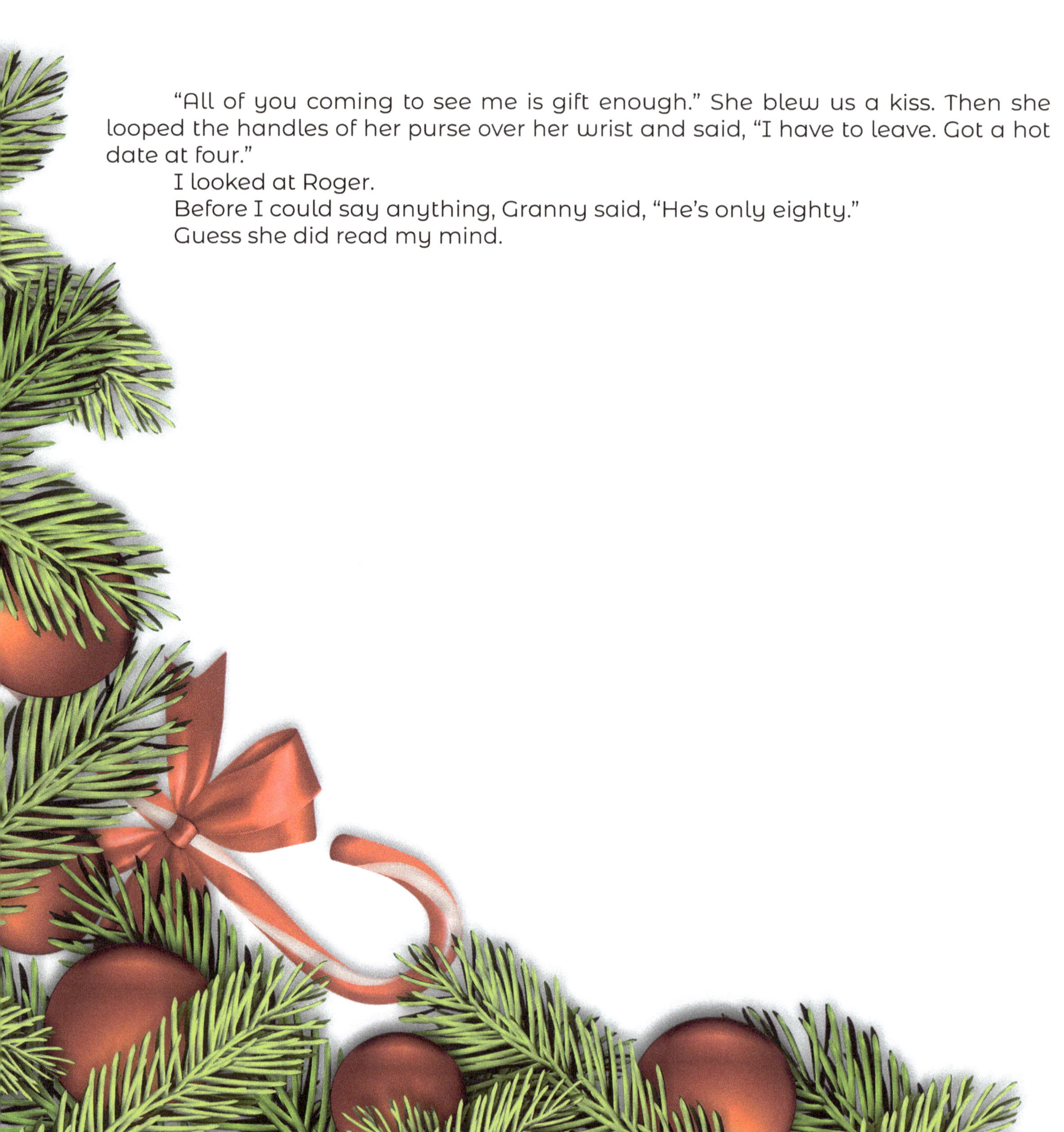

"All of you coming to see me is gift enough." She blew us a kiss. Then she looped the handles of her purse over her wrist and said, "I have to leave. Got a hot date at four."

I looked at Roger.

Before I could say anything, Granny said, "He's only eighty."

Guess she did read my mind.

# Poetry

by Susan York Meyers

A Christmas of white
May be your delight
But if there's no snow
Settle for lights all aglow
Merry Christmas to all
Whether big or small
May loved ones be near
And the day bring good cheer!

Mistletoe delight
Kisses by the firelight
Santa's grownup treat

Snow falling
In a slow frosty dance
Calm
White
Beautiful

Christmas Day arrived
Neatly wrapped now ripped and gone
Friends, food, and love shared

Merry Christmas
from
Woolsey and Granny!

Deck the cave with poison berries

Fa la la la la, la la la la

Wrap the tree with twinkling fairies

Fa la la la la, la la la la

Don we now our warmest woolies

Fa la la la la, la la la la

Trolls and Yaks and knitted booties

Fa la la la la, la la la la

See the book, Grrr...Night!, by Susan York Meyers, illustrated by Marla F. Jones

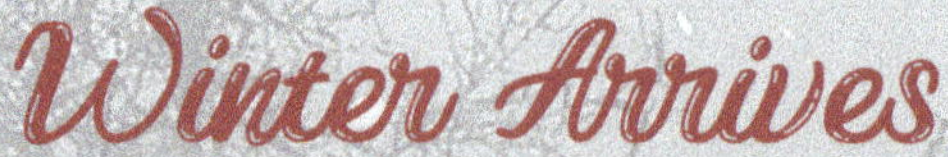

# Winter Arrives

by Howard F. Stein, Light and Shadow


Winter declared itself today
with rude finality.
Relentless cold rain and wind
tore the last reluctant leaves
from scrawny scrub oak.
Bare branches cut spectral figures
against the gray, bone-chilling afternoon.

Heedless of any calendar,
winter stole the stage.
"I arrive when I please,"
winter decreed to its shivering audience,
who put on their heavy coats
and left the theater
for biting wind, howling trees,
and a perilous trip home.

It was a simple matter
of who was sovereign,
and who was subject.

# In Search of Light:
## A Christmas Poem

Day dims early;
Darkness engulfs.
We dream of light
That might dispel the night.

We watch for signs
Among the stars;
We stand vigil
In the dark.

We lie down
In hope of morning gifts --
We kill over the naming
Of the light.

We are united
By the winter night.


by Howard F. Stein

# A Truck, A Tree, and a Christmas Wish

by M. Jane Hawkins

Myra's mother didn't complain during the day. "I feel like a walking furnace," she told Myra. "I hope this baby comes soon." But when the sun went down, her internal heater couldn't keep up with the single-digit breezes whipping into the house.

"Well, that does it." Daddy pushed the last towel in the house under the door trying to keep the cold wind from creeping in. Every dish towel, bath towel, wash cloth, and rag was crammed into cracks around windows and doors.

Myra loved her momma. Loved her more than her "Blanky." So Myra took her blanket and gave it to her mother.

"Oh, sugar, how sweet," Momma said as she kissed Myra's cheek. "This is just what I need. Thank you."

Myra swallowed hard. She wanted to bring up the Christmas tree again. She had to convince her parents that they absolutely must get a tree. But they had already told her there would be no tree and no packages. "A new baby brother or sister will be our gift," her parents said. With their growing family and the hospital bills that would follow the new baby home, spending money on a tree and presents was out of the question.

Myra was happy about the baby. But she knew her parents wouldn't have to worry about gifts if only they had a tree. Santa would take care of that. Myra stood at the window and thought, Christmas will be so boring with no tree and no packages. Just today all over again.

Then a red truck zoomed by. Ever since the weather turned cold and the snow and ice came, the same red truck drove down her road helping neighbors whose cars had slid into the ditch. Sometimes the truck beeped at Myra when he rushed by. Sometimes, to her surprise, he winked at her. Lately, he played Christmas music.

"If Santa drove a truck instead of a sleigh, it would surely look like that one. I bet he works for Santa," Myra thought.

"What are you doing, honey?" asked Daddy when he saw her standing at the window with her eyes closed.

"Making a wish," she said.

"What are you wishing for?" he asked.

"That the red truck would bring us a Christmas tree. I have a feeling he works for Santa."

Daddy didn't answer.

Suddenly, Momma called from the kitchen. "It's time," she said. "We'd better get to the hospital."

"I'll get the truck," answered Daddy. He rushed out the door—and hurried back in. "The snow's too deep. I'll never get the truck out."

"This baby is in a hurry," Momma said, her voice tinged with fear.

From her station at the window, Myra squealed, "It's the red truck! And he's coming to our house! Santa sent him, I just know it." She ran to the door and flung it open just in time to see a young man and Momma's doctor climb out of the red truck. The truck smiled at Myra as the radio blasted "Here Comes Santa Claus."

"I'm Frank," said the young man. "Tony's my truck. Tony and I were doing our regular run. We usually come by here last, but Tony insisted we come this way first. We spotted the doc here in the ditch."

"I had a feeling that your baby was coming tonight," said the doctor.

Myra waited in the kitchen with Daddy and Frank while the doctor helped Momma deliver the baby. They heard the truck beeping and beeping.

"I'd better go see what Tony wants," said Frank.

"Did he say the truck wants something?" Daddy asked Myra.

"I want to go see," Myra yelled. "Please, Daddy, please."

"OK, honey, but put your coat on."

Myra threw on her raggedy coat and hurried out the door. She stomped through the snow, leaving a trail of mittens and her stocking cap. But when she got to Tony, Myra froze, just like the icicles hanging from the porch roof.

"Tony, this is Myra," said Frank.

Tony smiled. Then Myra smiled and her tears dried. Tony beeped and Myra giggled.

"Want to sit inside?" asked Frank.

"Oh yes, please."

Tony's door swung open and the radio played "Have Yourself a Merry Little Christmas." With a boost from Frank, Myra climbed into the truck and clutched the steering wheel. Tony bounced and Myra laughed. Tony beeped and Myra clapped. Sitting inside Tony was like getting a big hug.

"Oh, I almost forgot," said Frank. He went to the back of the truck and pulled out the biggest Christmas tree Myra had ever seen. And, it was decorated!

Frank handed her a package wrapped in reindeer paper and topped with a giant red bow. "Can you carry this?"

"My wish came true," Myra shouted all the way to the house and into her parents' bedroom. "Momma, Daddy, look what the red truck brought us. I told you he was Santa's helper."

"Look what we got for Christmas," said Daddy. He sat by Momma, who was holding Myra's new baby sister wrapped in Myra's blanky.

"What was all that noise outside?" asked Momma. "And what's going on in the kitchen?"

"Come look," said Myra. "You can bring the baby."

Everyone laughed.

The tree stood in front of the window where Myra had spent so many hours. Boxes filled with warm coats for everyone - even the baby - were under the tree. A special box with Myra's name held a new blanket and lots of books. The smell of a freshly roasted turkey came from the kitchen.

Grateful tears filled Momma's eyes. "Oh my stars!"

"Where did all this come from?" asked Daddy.

"Santa," squealed Myra.

"I've gotta' go," said Frank. "Tony's getting cold and we have more rounds to make. Let's go, Doc. Merry Christmas everyone."

Momma and the new baby huddled by the stove. Daddy pulled a bite off the juicy turkey. Myra squeezed behind the tree, her face pressed against the window. "Thank you, Tony," she whispered.

Tony winked, and with a "Ho Ho Ho" he dashed out of sight.

# Kat & Tanya's Christmas Story

by K. J. Williams

*Chapter 1*

My sister and I lay on our stomachs gazing out the oversized window at the head of our bed. With Christmas Eve magic, the moon cast a golden path across the glittering snow.

"Kat, I'm eight this year," I said.  "I can stay awake longer than you. I'll see Santa. You won't."

Kat frowned. "Six-year-olds don't get sleepy on Christmas Eve. I'll hear him, too. The reindeer's feet will clop on the roof and the sleigh will go kerplop!"

"What are you talking about?" I propped myself up on my elbows. "Santa will land in the front yard 'cause we don't have a fireplace, duh."

"No." Kat chewed her lip. "People would see him. It's faster sliding down chimneys."

 "How does he do it when there is no chimney, like at our house?"

"He comes through the heater pipes," Kat said. "He snaps his fingers and magically appears in a puff of rainbow smoke."

"You're crazy." I raised my voice. "His magic reindeer dust only works on reindeers to make the sleigh fly."

"Girls!" Daddy yelled from the living room. "Don't make me come in there. Santa won't leave gifts until you're both asleep."

We slid down under the covers. "Santa and the reindeer always land on the roofs," Kat whispered. "The sleigh bump might wake us up."

"No, we'll find footprints and hoofprints in our snowy front yard, in the morning," I whispered back.

*Chapter 2*

Kat and I didn't get along during the weeks before Christmas. Our first fight was how to decorate the Christmas tree.

"Hurry up, Kat," I said. "Just throw the stringy tinsel on the tree."

"It's prettier if you separate each strand," she said. "Then it hangs down and shimmers like silver icicles."

"That takes forever. I want to watch a Christmas movie." I made a pile of the empty Christmas decoration boxes by the kitchen snack bar where Momma was listening to Christmas songs and signing cards. Daddy looked relaxed, kicked back in his recliner reading the newspaper.

"I want it to look sparkly," Kat said.

"Here, I'll speed it up." I grabbed a fistful out of her hand and launched the tinsel clump into the branches.

"Stop, Tanya!" Kat yelled. "You're making it ugly!"

"What's the problem, girls?" Daddy looked over his newspaper.

"She's messing up the tree!" Kat stomped her foot.

"Hey, I'm just decorating my way," I said. "She can decorate her way."

"That's enough girls," Daddy said. "Both of you are done. Go to your room."

Cookie decorating was our favorite tradition. Momma never yelled at us for messing up the kitchen. We rolled out the dough and cut out the shapes. But this year, Kat kept hogging the Santa cookie cutter.

"It's my turn," I said. "You've cut out a whole pan of Santas." I grabbed for it.

"I only want Santa cookies!" Kat held it behind her back.

"Why? That's stupid." I reached around her.

"Because Santa likes them best." Kat ran around the kitchen table, keeping the cookie cutter just out of reach.

"Give it to me!" I chased her between the chairs. "Santa doesn't like them best because he would be eating himself, dumb dumb." I tackled her as she tried to escape to the living room.

"AHHH, help me, Momma!" Kat screamed. "Tanya's killing me!"

I sat on Kat's stomach as I pried one finger at a time from the cookie cutter.

"What are you girls doing?" Momma pulled me off my sister.

"I'm not done with this cookie cutter, yet!" Kat whined.

"She's hogging the Santa!" I shoved my hair out of my face with flour-coated hands.

"You look like a skunk." Kat jumped up and kept the table between us. "Skunk hair, skunk hair! Tanya's got skunk hair!"

"That's it!" Momma held out her palm for the Santa cookie cutter. "You're both done. I'll finish the cutting and baking, you two wash up, then go play outside to cool off." Momma ignored us as she put a pan in the oven. "We'll do the decorating later."

I stomped out the back door and sat on a swing, dragging my feet in the dirt. Kat plopped down on the side of the sandbox, making a finger trail in the sand.

I broke the silence. "I'm bored. Let's play horses and race around bushes." The sun warmed my face and my legs wanted to run.

"Nah, I want to play in the sandbox," she said.

"You never want to play what I want." I kicked a rock.

"You don't ever let ME pick!" she yelled.

"Because I'm the oldest," I shot back. "So, I'm in charge."

"The smartest should pick." Kat kept making designs in the sand. "Everybody knows that's me." I wanted to slap her! I jumped off the swing and paced around the yard. I noticed the shed near the woods.

"Okay, smarty pants, let's make a bet. We both have to look through the peep hole in the shed." I pointed to the back of our lot. "Whoever can keep their eye up to the hole the longest, wins."

"Then the winner gets to choose what we play?"

"You got it! You in?" I dared her.

"But it's off-limits. If we get caught, we'll be in big trouble."

Our parents had repeatedly reminded us that the rickety shed was owned by the church next to our house. It was not ours, so don't touch! If that wasn't enough to keep us away, they pointed out the tall summer grass was the perfect hiding place for snakes.

"Don't you want to know what's in there," I taunted, "or are you chicken?"

"Am not!" Kat dusted the sand from her hands. "At least the snakes aren't out in winter."

We spit into our palms and shook on it.

*Chapter 3*

I got the ladder out of the garage, careful not to make noise. We snuck around to the back. From our yard, the shed's peeling paint camouflaged it among the overgrown trees and clingy vines. I propped the ladder up against a side wall just below a rotted-out knot hole, where we could take a peek.

"I'll go first." Kat climbed.

"I'll start counting," I said, "when you put your eye up next to the hole."

She faced the hole, took a deep breath and tucked her hair behind her ears.

"Okay, count." She looked in.

"One, two, three," I counted.

"AH!" Kat jerked back from the knothole, trembling so hard the ladder shook.

"What is it?" I yelled up to her.

"An eyeball!" She jumped off the ladder and ran back toward the house.

"An eye? Like an evil eye?" All I heard was the slam of the backdoor. I hesitated at the bottom of the ladder. I had to see. I climbed. With each step, I tried to convince myself it was nothing. My sister was just a scaredy cat.

At the top, I peered into the peep hole. Not one, but two eyes stared back at me! I gasped and jerked back. The ladder tipped. I tried to jump off, but my hands were frozen. I did a sideways face plant on the ground. I couldn't breathe.

"Tanya, what have you done to your sister?" Momma's voice came from the back porch. "Where are you?"

I realized that the ladder and I lay hidden in the weeds. Probably surrounded by snakes.

"You better not be hiding! You're in big trouble. You have five minutes to get in this house and explain why you're scaring your little sister."

I stumbled to the house and made up a story about us doing gymnastic tricks off the old propane tank. That was a no-no, too, so Momma sentenced us to two-days of cleaning. We had to wash all the windows in the house and clean the garage. I imagined we would've had to clean the bathrooms if Momma knew we'd been hanging around the shed.

By Christmas Eve day we were on our last chore...cleaning the garage. Kat stopped sweeping.

"What do you think is in the shed?" she whispered.

"A white face with creepy eyes." I moved boxes.

"A dead body?" Kat chewed her bottom lip.

"Nah, unless someone just died, it would be a skeleton," I said.

"Whatever it is, I'm not going back there," Kat said.

"We could ask Momma." I sat down on a dusty lawn chair.

"No way," Kat said. "Then she'd know we were messing around back there."

## Chapter 4

"Do you hear something?" Kat turned toward the closed garage door.

"It's just the wind, rattling the door," I said. "What's the matter? You worried the shed ghost is haunting us?" I giggled.

"Shush!" Kat dropped her broom and walked closer to the door. I joined her. A faint yell came from outside. I pushed the garage door opener.

I saw something more terrifying than what was in the shed. Our car rolling backwards in slow motion down the driveway. No one was in the driver's seat. The wheels were angled making the car back up in a tight curve. The driver's door swung open. The car stopped in the street, but still facing the driveway.

That's when we saw Daddy sprawled on the ground, face down. Not moving. We both stood there stunned, afraid he was dead.

"I need help!" he yelled.

We ran to him.

"Tell Mom I can't get up," he said.

"I'll go." Kat took off like a rabbit.

"Daddy, you okay?" I said. "Let me roll you onto your back." I pushed his shoulder over so he could look up at me, he moaned in pain.

"I think something is broken," he said breathing heavy. "Need to...go...to ...the hospital."

I wiped my tears with the back of my hand. "Dad, are you dying?" I choked out.

"Don't...worry." He paused to breathe. "The car...rolled backwards....after I...got out. Tried to.... jump back in....to stop it.... door knocked me down."

Momma ran to us and dropped to her knees. "Here, Tanya, the 911 operator is on my cell phone." She forced the phone into my hand. "Give them our address." Momma stroked Daddy's rumpled hair and asked him where he'd been hurt.

I gave the operator directions to our house, along with Momma and Daddy's names, then I hung onto the phone like a lifeline.

My sister and I each held one of Dad's hands as our tears ran like rivers.

"The ambulance is on the way, honey. Don't move," Mom said.

"Don't die, Daddy," Kat begged.

"Get to...the car... and put it...in park," Dad croaked out. "It could... roll back into the driveway...over us."

Momma parked the car in front of the house.

The sirens made goosebumps pop out on my arms. This couldn't be happening. It was Christmas Eve! Kat and I hugged as the paramedics loaded Daddy into the ambulance. Our neighbor, everyone called Grandma Beryl, came over and offered to stay with us while Momma went to the hospital.

## Chapter 5

Grandma Beryl led us back into our house. In the kitchen she offered us all the Christmas cookies we could eat, along with mugs of hot chocolate with whipped cream. I nibbled at a cookie without even tasting it.

"Daddy's got to be okay. It's almost Christmas." I couldn't imagine Christmas without Daddy stretched out in his recliner smiling as we opened our gifts.

"Don't you know Christmas is the time for miracles?" Grandma Beryl asked.

"I thought it was the time for Santa and the reindeers," Kat said sniffling.

"That too, but a lot of amazing things happen on Jesus's birthday." Grandma Beryl offered Kat a tissue.

"Like some sort of Christmas magic?" I asked.

"Yes, God likes to give us gifts in honor of his Son's birthday," Grandma Beryl said.

"Since God and Jesus are up in their sky mansion," Kat said, "Jesus can't blow out his candles. We give each other Christmas presents, instead of birthday presents, right?"

"Yes, that's right," Grandma Beryl said. "You're a smart one."

"I told you." Kat tapped her head.

I rolled my eyes at her.

"But Jesus can give us presents too, just not wrapped ones. Let's ask Him for a one now." Grandma Beryl linked our hands in hers and bowed her head. She prayed for our Daddy to be okay.

While Grandma Beryl bustled around the kitchen making a casserole for supper, Kat and I wandered out to the backyard and sat on the swings.

"I hate waiting," Kat said, dragging her heels in the grass.

"Same here. I keep seeing Daddy on the ground hurting." I eased the swing back and forth with my feet.

"There's nothing to do," Kat said. "I'm so bored."

"Hey, I know." I said. "Let's go check out the shed. Whatever is in there, can't be as bad as Daddy's accident."

"I'm not scared anymore," Kat said.

We walked back to the ladder, still hidden in the weeds. I propped it back up under our peep hole.

"Let's try the door." Kat marched to the front of the shed.

"Isn't it locked?" I asked.

"Just a rusty deadbolt. Help me pull it back."

We planted our feet and pulled together. It sounded like fingernails scraping on a chalkboard. After a couple of tries, it slid back. We looked at each other.

"Oldest goes first," Kat said, with a grin.

"No, you were right," I said. "The smartest should go first."  We giggled.

"I dare you," Kat said.

"I double dare you," I said.

Neither of us moved.

"Forget it. Let's do it together," Kat said.

We jerked the door open.

*Chapter 6*

Our jaws dropped.

"Statues? Seriously?" Kat walked in the door. "They're taller than me."

"That's not saying much, shorty." I elbowed her. "But they're grown up size."

A group of old statues, draped in cobwebs were crowded into the small shed.

A shaft of sunlight shot through the peep hole and lit up the pale face we'd seen. It was a man with shoulder-length hair, wearing a long, faded blue robe and sandals. Next to him was a woman wearing a head covering. She was kneeling next to an animal trough.

"Hey look what I found" Kat said. "A baby wrapped in a towel." She squeezed between the statues and wiped the dust off the baby's face with her shirt tail.

I hit my forehead with my palm. "They're part of a nativity scene."

"Oh, like baby Jesus, Mary and Joseph?" Kat asked.

"Yeah, like with the straw and the farm animals people put in their yards at Christmas," I explained. "Because it was Jesus' birthday!"

"Because Jesus was born in a barn, not a hospital. We talked about this in my church class." Kat's eyes lit up. "Let's set them up in our front yard as a surprise for Daddy when he gets home."

"But these statues don't belong to us," I said.

"The church people aren't using them," Kat argued, "or they would have come got them already since tomorrow's Christmas."

"You're right," I agreed. "They probably have new ones now. These are old. Let's ask for a Christmas miracle, first." I took Kat's hand and we knelt down on the dirty floor by the manger. I wasn't sure what to say, so I just started talking. "Jesus, it's your birthday. But we need a present for our hurt Daddy." I couldn't talk anymore because a lump was in my throat, like stuck mashed potatoes.

Kat squeezed my hand. "Grandma Beryl told us you like to give us gifts at Christmas, too," Kat continued. "Jesus, if you could sprinkle down some Christmas magic to make our Daddy better? That would be the best present, ever."

Grandma Beryl and her two grandsons helped us drag the statues out of the shed. Kat sprayed them with Momma's dish soap. I rinsed them off with the hose. We dried and polished them until their crackly faces glowed. We left the shepherds and three old guys with crowns in the back of the shed, because we were too tired to pull them out.

## Chapter 7

Just at dusk, when the street lights came on, Momma brought Daddy home with his arm in a sling. Grandma Beryl, Kat and I ran out to meet them as soon as we heard the car drive up. Daddy had a broken shoulder. I hugged him on his good side while Kat danced around like a hyper elf.

"Are we still opening presents, tonight?" Kat asked.

"Sure," Daddy said. "After all it's Christmas Eve tradition. I'm fine."

"What's this?" Momma asked as she stopped in front of our manger scene.

"Don't be upset, Momma," I begged. "We were so worried about Daddy, we had to do something, so we looked in the shed. We saw baby Jesus, Mary and Joseph so we set up this nativity scene for you guys and prayed for Jesus to send us a special Christmas gift."

"We wanted to surprise you," Kat chimed in.

Momma shook her finger at us. "You girls are ruler-breakers!" Her frown faded into a smile. "I'll make an exception since it's Christmas." Momma put her arm around Daddy to help him in the house.

"Did you get your Christmas present from Jesus?" Daddy asked.

"Yeah," we both said at the same time. We hooked our pinky fingers and yelled, "Jinx!" Like we always did.

"What was it?" Daddy grimaced as he slumped into a kitchen chair.

"You, Daddy!" I said.

"You're our present! You got to come home. Jesus sprinkled some Christmas magic down on us," Kat said.

We high-fived.

Momma and Daddy thanked Grandma Beryl After she left, we munched down on the casserole. Kat and I got done first and then fidgeted as our parents took their time.

"You done?" I hovered at Daddy's good elbow.

Kat cleared our dishes.

"In a hurry, girls?" Daddy teased taking one last bite in slow motion. We couldn't open presents until after supper. It was a family tradition. Kat and I set a new dish washing speed record.

When we gathered around the Christmas tree, Kat read the tags and I passed out gifts to everyone. We pretended to be Santa's little helpers. We both got Barbie dolls with extra outfits and the usual; socks, panties and books.

After we opened all our gifts, Kat and I set out the Christmas cookies for Santa and carrots for the reindeer. We argued about where Santa would park the sleigh until Dad yelled at us to go to sleep.

*Chapter 8*

I opened my eyes and listened to Kat snore.  "Rats! I fell asleep." I crawled over the pillow and looked out at the diamonds dancing on the snow in the early morning sun. No sleigh tracks. No reindeer hoof prints. I hoped Kat was right and Santa landed on the roof. I pressed my nose to the frosty glass, my breath steamed it up. In my best printing I wrote, Merry Christmas!

"Wake up!" I shook my sister. "Let's go see what Santa brought."

"Wha...ugh." Kat groaned and rolled over. I flipped back the covers. "So cold," she mumbled curling up into a ball.

"Get up!" I jumped out of the bed and sprinted down the hall to our parent's room. We weren't allowed to see what Santa brought until Momma and Daddy came with us.

It took forever for Momma to help Daddy into his robe because of his injury. Then, they kept us prisoner in the kitchen while the coffee brewed. Finally, we walked into the living room to see Santa's gifts.

Toys sat organized under the tree. I scuttled around looking at which tags said Kat, and which said Tanya. I counted. Yep, we both had the same amount, except for one doll that looked like a tiny real-life girl. She had moveable arms, legs and eyelids. She was dressed in a silky red ruffled dress covered in lace with sparkles glittering through it. I picked her up looking for a tag, but there wasn't one.

"Is that yours?" Kat frowned.

"It doesn't have a tag, but I'm sure she's mine." I twirled a long blonde curl around my finger.

"How do you know?" Kat squinted. "It's probably mine, 'cause I'm the youngest."

"But this is a big girl doll," I explained. "If it was a baby doll, it would be yours."

"No, because I'm not a baby." Kat crossed her arms and scooted closer.

"Look at your toys." I tried to distract her from the doll. "You got lots of good stuff.”

She never took her eyes off the doll.

“Let me see her.” Kat reached for her. I blocked the doll with my body.

“No, I found her first,” I argued. “She’s mine.”

“Let me hold her!” Kat grabbed the doll’s arm.

I jerked back. “Let go!”

I had one arm and she had the other.

“Let me have her!” Kat yelled.

In a flash we were having a doll tug-of-war. Momma jumped up from her chair but was too slow. The doll’s arm broke off at the shoulder. I fell backwards with the doll. Kat fell the opposite way holding an arm. She burst into hysterical tears.

“You broke her, Tanya!” Kat screamed.

“It’s your fault!” I yelled.

“Girls!” Momma sat down cross-legged between us. “It’s Christmas. There will be no fighting on Christmas.”  She pulled us each under one arm.  “Maybe Santa forgot to write the tag, but I bet he meant for you both to share the doll.”

From across the room, Daddy burst out laughing. We turned and stared at him. Laughing? I was expecting him to punish us.

“I don’t think this is funny, dear.” Momma frowned.

Daddy was laughing so hard, he couldn’t talk. He pointed to his shoulder sling. Then I understood and I grinned.

“Daddy is telling us is that this doll is like him,” I explained. “She has a broken shoulder, too!”

“You’re right, but she didn’t get run over by a car,” Kat said.

“No, but we can play ambulance and bandage her up like Daddy,” I said.

Daddy winked at us. We giggled as we took turns holding her.

“Let’s promise to never fight over her again,” I said.

“Pinky swear?”  Kat held out her hooked little finger. We shook on it.

“I’ll get some bandages.” I rushed to the bathroom for Band-Aids.

“I’ll set up a hospital bed for her and get our medical kit.” Kat took off for our toy box.

Momma found some paper face masks. We played doctor and surgeon the rest of Christmas break. The doll reminded us of our most precious present, our miracle Christmas gift from Jesus, our Daddy.

# Two Old Ladies and Santa Claus

by Susan York Meyers

Annabelle paused in the doorway of the Good Times Thrift Store and stomped her feet. Snow flew off her boots.

"Excuse me," Lillybelle said from behind her.

"I don't want to track snow into the store," Annabelle explained.

"And I don't want to freeze to death. Move."

Christmas bells chimed as the door shut behind them. One last stomp and Annabelle eagerly headed toward the used book section.

"I'll join you in a moment," Lillybelle called after her.

Annabelle paused. "Where are you going?"

"I'm going to check out that rack of housedresses."

"Whatever for?"

"To wear, Sister. What else?"

Annabelle trailed behind Lillybelle. "But, housedresses are what old people wear. You'll look old."

Reaching the rack, Lillybelle examined a yellow check dress. "This looks nice. And, I am seventy-two. The secret is out that I'm old. Besides, I just want a few to wear around the house. It's not like I'm going to turn up at Ladies' Bible Class in one."

Annabelle tugged on Lillybelle's sleeve. "Sister..."

Lillybelle snorted. "Really, Annabelle..."

"There's Tori Mitchell. Let's go say hello." The younger woman stood a few feet away staring at a Santa suit hanging on the wall. "Ho, ho, ho," Annabelle said cheerfully. To her surprise, Tori's blue eyes filled with tears. "Why, Sweetie, what's wrong?"

Tori sniffed. "Don't worry about me. I'm being a big baby."

Lillybelle handed her a tissue.  "Can we help?"

Tori blew her nose. "My husband used to dress up as Santa. He'd hide behind the house, and I'd make up some pretense to get Tucker to look out the back window. He'd catch "Santa" sneaking away. Kyle got such a kick out of playing Santa. This is Tucker's first Christmas without his dad. I hate that he's going to lose Santa too."

"I'm so sorry," Annabelle said. She gave Tori a hug.

"It's okay. There are certainly more important things to worry about. I guess Christmas Eve has brought out the waterworks in me." The sisters watched Tori walk away, hunched and dejected.

"We've got to help," Annabelle said.

"How?"

"One of us will play Santa tonight," Annabelle stated firmly.

Lillybelle gasped. "What?"

Annabelle patted her sister on the back. "We'll buy this suit, dress up and let Tucker catch Santa."

"But, Sister, we're women." Lillybelle cleared her throat.

Annabelle laughed. "Haven't you heard? Nowadays women can do anything. Even play Santa in a pinch."

Later that evening, the sisters stood in front of Annabelle's quilt covered bed. Lillybelle fingered the red fabric of the coat. "Did you talk to Tori?"

Annabelle nodded. "She and Tucker will be home tonight."

"Well, I guess we need to decide who wears it."

"Obviously, I'm too tall for the suit," Annabelle said. "Besides, your figure, er, fits it better."

Lillybelle stuck her tongue out. "Ho, ho, ho." It took a lot of pushing and pulling and the addition of a pillow, but Lillybelle finally resembled Santa.

Annabelle eyed her. "At least the street light will be some distance away."

"I can barely walk in these boots," Lillybelle grumbled.

"Just be careful going down the stairs. We don't want kids reading in the paper tomorrow about Santa breaking her neck."

Lillybelle shook her head. "Kids don't read papers anymore.

"True, they'd watch it on You Tube."

Outside, the sisters picked and shuffled their way through the snow. "You look very festive," Annabelle said. "You know, maybe we should pin a sprig of holly to your hat."

"Try it and you'll get coal in your stocking," Lillybelle shot back. They managed to reach Tucker's house without losing the pillow or breaking an ankle.

Annabelle straightened Lillybelle's hat. "Isn't this exciting? I'll call Tori. She'll get Tucker to the window. Then you can stroll behind the house. I'll meet you on the other side."

"As we planned," Lillybelle said. "Alzheimer's hasn't gotten me yet."

Lillybelle waited as Annabelle phoned. After a moment, Annabelle grinned and gave her a thumbs up. Lillybelle slung Santa's black sack over her shoulder and stomped forward. Every other step her left boot came dangerously close to slipping off and in places where the snow had turned to slush, she slipped and slid. "My sister and her harebrained ideas," she muttered. "Why – "

"Santa!" a joyful voice rang out. Lillybelle glanced over her shoulder. Tucker's grin stretched from ear to ear. He waved. She waved back and hurried forward. She put a finger to her lips. He nodded. Okay, maybe not such a harebrained idea. Huffing and puffing, she reached the side of the house.

Annabelle squashed Lillybelle in a big hug. "You did it!"

"And he'll know it if you don't hush."

Annabelle laughed and took Lillybelle's arm. "Come on, Santa. It's time to get you home to your new housecoat and your old rocker."

"Miss Annabelle?" The whisper made them both jump. The sisters turned. Tucker hung out his bedroom window, hair tousled and out of breath.

"Hello, Tucker," Annabelle said as Lillybelle hastened to straighten her beard.

"Thanks, Miss Annabelle. Thanks, Miss Lillybelle."

"I'm not Lillybelle, I'm…"

"Hush," Annabelle said. "He's seven, Sister, not an idiot."

Lillybelle grimaced at the little boy. "I guess I'm not a very convincing Santa."

He grinned back. "Sure you are. But last year I asked Daddy if Santa Claus was real and he told me the truth.  Man-to-man." Tucker's voice caught.

"But your mother thinks you still believe," Annabelle said.

He nodded. "Daddy said Mama still believes, so we kept the secret." He jiggled up and down in his excitement. "She's not ready to know the truth yet."

"We understand perfectly," Annabelle exclaimed.

"Don't tell her," Tucker warned.

"Oh, we won't," Lillybelle assured him. "Cross our hearts." And they did.

Annabelle took Lillybelle's arm. "Goodnight, Tucker."

"'Night!"

"And we wonder why Jesus tells us to become like little children," Lillybelle said as they trudged across the snow to their cozy home.

"I'm glad we could help," Annabelle said. "I wonder if his mom still believes in the Easter Bunny."

# A Christmas Kerfuffle

by Marla F. Jones

I scurried about putting the finishing touches on the food for our family Christmas Eve party at Mom's house. My son-in-law and daughter wrapped the last gift, leaving a mess of paper scraps, tape and boxes. My husband and granddaughter loaded all the gifts and goodies into the car and, finally, seatbelts on, we opened the garage door and  backed  out into the street. The headlights shone brightly in the early, December evening.

Pointing to a car parked in front of our neighbor's house, my granddaughter asked, "Nanna, who's that?"

"I think our neighbor is having a Christmas party. See all the cars in her driveway?" Then to my husband I said, "We'd better hurry. I need to stop at the grocery store on the way to Mom's. I have to pick up a few last minute ingredients for my dessert."

A few minutes later, he dropped me off at the entrance,  and I ran inside and joined other last minute shoppers. I was tossing nuts and whipped cream into the cart when my cell phone rang. "Hello?"

"Is everything okay?" asked my mother.

"Oh, yes, we're just running a bit late. I had to pick up a few things. We'll be there in a few minutes!"

"Well, alright...See you in a bit."

Drats! I thought. Everyone is waiting on us! I scurried through the check-out line and out to the car where my family waited, warm and cozy, ready to celebrate Christmas Eve at Grandma's.

When I climbed into the car, my husband grumbled, "Jenna called. She's running a little late." Everyone chuckled. Late was normal for Jenna.

We pulled onto the highway, humming along with Christmas carols on the radio, our tummies rumbling in anticipation of Christmas goodies.

When we arrived, the porch light was off but we could see the television glowing inside.

"Dad must have forgotten to turn on the Christmas lights," I said. "Everyone help carry in the gifts and food!" Arms full, we hurried through the bitter cold and rang the doorbell.

No answer.

A tiny, niggling feeling percolated in the bottom of my stomach. I pushed the doorbell again.

No answer.

"Why isn't Grandpa answering the door?" my daughter asked.

A fuzzy, disconnected scene unfolded in my brain. Then, that feeling in my stomach welled to a full-blown ache. "Uh, oh...I think I might have told Mom we would have the party at our house."

"You're kidding, right?" asked my husband.

I grabbed my phone and dialed. "Mom, where are you and Dad?"

"We're in front of your house," she answered. "Where are you?"

I groaned. "We're on your front porch."

Mom chuckled. "I thought something was wrong. We saw all of you get in your car and leave. Don't you remember at Thanksgiving you volunteered to host the Christmas Eve get-together?"

The forgotten memory shoved its way forward, like a battering ram, from the back of my brain. I **had** agreed to host the Christmas party! "We'll be there as quick as we can." I hung up the phone and yelled, "Hurry! Load everything back in the car! We're going back to our house."

Inside the car my husband rolled his eyes and shook his head. Everyone else fought back snickers and giggles. Needless to say, I was not laughing. I was mortified! I know I'm a bit forgetful, but this took the cake!

A few minutes later we pulled back into our driveway. And there, parked in front of our house, waiting patiently, were Mom and Dad, my brother and sister-in-law and their kids. They had been waiting *forty-five minutes* for us to come back from the grocery store!

Everyone did their best to keep a straight face as they carried gifts and food into the mess of wrapping paper scraps, tape and boxes, dust, and dirty dishes. They didn't want to make me feel worse than I already did. But my brother, never able to resist a good-humored jab, fought back a grin, and asked, "Want me to vacuum, sis?" I glared at him. Then he asked, "By the way, where's Jenna?"

I hurdled a pile of presents like a long distance runner, rushed to the telephone and dialed, visions of Jenna arriving at my parent's darkened house swirling in my head. Unable  to refrain, someone giggled. Then, everyone started laughing. We laughed until tears ran down our faces.

Needless to say, we now triple-check all our holiday plans.

**kerfuffle**
*noun*
Brit.*informal*
noun: kerfuffle;   plural noun: kerfuffles
1. a commotion or fuss, esp. one caused by conflicting views.

## Glori Alexander, illustrator

Glori loves bold colors and bold flavors. She has illustrated over 2 dozen children's books, including *Space Station Vacation*. You can find her design and illustration at www.behance.net/glorialexander and on Instagram @glori_draws.

## David Barrow, illustrator

David Barrow worked as a graphic designer, camera man and video editor. In 2016, Barrow embarked on his lifelong dream of illustrating children's books. Barrow has illustrated ten books to date.

## Darlina Eichman, author

Darlina Chambers Eichman enjoyed her educational career as a science teacher and curriculum developer. She taught children in grades K-9 and, at the graduate level, taught teachers how to incorporate space (under NASA grants) into their classrooms. In addition, Darlina developed and delivered on-line training programs to large businesses and the Federal Aviation Administration.

### M. Jane Hawkins, author

M. Jane Hawkins has been a junior high school English teacher, a stay-at-home mom, and a part-time employee at a regional running magazine where she sold advertisements, wrote and edited articles and eventually became editor. She has been a reading mentor for children and helped start a newspaper club in an elementary school.

### Marla F. Jones, author and illustrator

Marla F. Jones has read thousands of children's books. Literally. As a first grade teacher, story time was her favorite part of the day. Marla illustrates with a colorful mix of media. She uses papers, fabrics and found objects, layering them to create texture and dimension to her folk art style.

### Sandra Byrd Lawson, author

Sandra Byrd Lawson grew up in rural Kentucky. As a little girl Lawson loved reading all types of books and exploring the hills and woods surrounding her home. She now lives in Oklahoma. Sandra writes chapter books and middle grade books.

### Susan York Meyers, author

Susan York Meyers is the author of books ranging from picture books to young adult novels. Her works include the award-winning picture book, *Grrr...Night!* In addition to her children's writing, Susan is also the author of *Two Little Old Ladies: It's all in the Attitude,* a humorous inspirational book combining both fiction and devotionals. You can find out more about Susan's books and her writing at susanameyers.com.

### Dorothy Shaw, author and illustrator

Dorothy Shaw grew up in Austin, Texas. She is an award-winning art director and graphic designer. Shaw is delighted to now be focusing on children's books illustration. Jerome the Stone is Shaw's debut as an author.

### Howard Stein, author

Howard F. Stein, Ph.D., an organizational, applied, psychoanalytic, medical anthropologist, psychohistorian, organizational consultant, and poet, is professor emeritus in the Department of Family and Preventive Medicine, University of Oklahoma Health Sciences Center, where he taught for 35 years. He is Poet Laureate of the High Plains Society for Applied Anthropology and author, co-author, or editor of thirty-two books.,

## Una Belle Townsend, author

Una Belle Townsend is retired from a career in teaching and library media. She has four books published through Pelican and six with Doodle and Peck Publishing. In 2007, Townsend was chosen to visit towns in Oklahoma with small populations who could not afford to have an author visit their library. As a former librarian, she enjoys reading to children and learning more about the great state of Oklahoma.

## Karen Williams, author

KJ Williams loves connecting kids to books. She spent thirty-seven years as a schoolteacher and media specialist encouraging children to discover and love books and reading. Camp Not Allowed, is Williams' debut book with Doodle and Peck Publishing.

## Barbara Shepherd, author

Barbara Shepherd is an award-winning writer, named the 2016 Rose State Outstanding Author and the ACW Writer of the Year. She is the 2019 PSO Poet Laureate and writes fiction, non-fiction, and poetry.

# Our Books

by K.J. Williams
illustrated by
Dorothy Shaw

by Una Belle Townsend
illustrated by
Vickie Kastl

by Una Belle Townsend
illustrated by David Barrow
(Scanner the Scottie series)

(Mila Denton series)
by Sandra Byrd Lawson



by Howard F. Stein

by Barbara Shepherd
illustrated by
David Barrow

by Darlina Eichman
illustrated by
Glori Alexander

by Susan York Meyers
illustrated by Marla Jones

written and illustrated by
Dorothy Shaw

by Susan York Meyers
cover design by Marla F. Jones

illustrated by Dorothy Shaw

written and illustrated
by Marla F. Jones

poetry and photographs
by Una Belle Townsend

by Una Belle Townsend
illustrated by Gwen
Coleman Lester

by Marla F. Jones
illustrated by
Holly Abston

by M. Jane Hawkins
illustrated by David Barrow

illustrated by David Barrow

For full descriptions and prices, visit
www.doodleandpeck.com

FROGGY BOTTOM BLUES
By Sharon Edge Martin
Illustrated by Timothy Lange

CAMPING WITH
BIGFOOT
Written by Matt Judkins
Illustrated by Kara M. Mitchell

The LITTLE OLD MAN,
the LITTLE OLD WOMAN,
and the LITTLE RED HEN
By David L. Roper
Illustrated by Kara Mitchell

Scarecrow's Journey
Written and Illustrated by Timothy Lange

THE BUFFALO
TRAIN RIDE
Desiree Morrison Webber
Static Illustrations by Sandy Shropshire

MY FRIEND,
FRANK
BY DAVID L. ROPER
ILLUSTRATED BY ADAM COBBLE

JUST PLAYING
By Anita Wadley Schladt
Illustrated by Hazel Conley

Doodle and Peck Publishing produces fun, family-friendly books, created by talented authors and illustrators. Most of our books have a curriculum connection, making them not just entertaining, but educational.

Many of our authors and illustrators visit schools and libraries sharing their passion for great literature. And last but not least, Doodle and Peck books are printed right here in the United States.

Contact information:
Doodle and Peck Publishing
P.O. Box 852105
Yukon, OK 73085

405.354.7422

www.doodleandpeck.com